T0114973

THE TEARS OF THE EARTH
Poems

John Ngong Kum Ngong

Langaa Research & Publishing CIG
Mankon, Bamenda

Publisher:
Langaa RPCIG
Langaa Research & Publishing Common Initiative Group
P.O. Box 902 Mankon
Bamenda
North West Region
Cameroon
Langaagrp@gmail.com
www.langaa-rpcig.net

Distributed in and outside N. America by African Books Collective
orders@africanbookscollective.com
www.africanbookscollective.com

ISBN-10: 9956-550-64-7

ISBN-13: 978-9956-550-64-7

Table of Contents

Foreword

More than a decade after the publication of his first collection of poems entitled **Walls of Agony**, and coming as the tenth in regular succession since the first, this new volume of poetry confirms John Ngong Kum Ngong as a bard of profound inspiration, diverse concerns; a visionary perception, and artistic activism crusading for "higher thoughts and nobler goals".

In this new volume of forty-seven poems, the poet, now at ease with a craft native to his deeper instincts, is deeply touched with noble anger at the plethora of ills that bedevil his society and beyond, especially the man-induced suicidal threat to his unique habitat – planet Earth.

The Tears of the Earth, without pretence, practically holds court for environmental or eco-concerns with global ripples. The poems particularly take to task the local Cameroonian/African and even global environmental policies impaled on the antlers of politics of interest, mal-governance and an insidious global materialistic culture. The volume stakes a legitimate claim as a landmark tributary to the mainstream discourse and current debates on global warming and climate change, especially by portraying Africa, still trapped and anaesthetized in the web of post-colonial vassalage, compelled to mortgage her natural resources for savage exploitation with little or no regard to either environmental impact or sustainability. The poems are an expression of the author's noble indignation at society's governing elite for allowing collective natural resources "Mother Earth' to be callously butchered, so ingloriously ransacked, liberally poisoned and gagged "Beyond Recognition" for mere lucre or "Midas' touch" which procures and sustains the infernal binary of "Power and Pride" deified by our societies.

Equally preoccupying is the poet's ire and disappointment at the tsunami of revolting social ills encouraged, by commission or omission, to luxuriate in and ruin our societies while virtue and other sane values are consciously pressed into languor or cynically trussed up for ridicule with dire consequences on the ecosphere and human welfare.

Confronted by this sombre situation, given his delicate sensitivity and energized poetic curiosity, the poet does not flounder in impotent denunciation, take refuge in a cul de sac nor bolt away in cowardice. He courageously espouses an activist but constructivist attitude – dissecting not to murder, but to diagnose and reconstruct. The dominantly regenerative and therapeutic potential represented by Mother Nature/ Earth in "Walking in the Woods", "In Love with Deep Waters", "Welcoming Nature", the grace, courage and inspiration exuded by the female gender in "Best Ever Maid", "Daring Women" and "Women of Heart", the constructivist moral tone in his satire and the relay posture in "The Need to Groom" speak volumes of the vision of hope in the collection even when the unassuming bard would have wafted, as he hopes to, "Out of the Red Zone".

The poems are cast in organic form and flow in free racy rhythms "uncorseted by regular patterns or restrictive rhyme scheme". Yet the poet is quite capable of achieving rare grace of form and cadence even in pieces with complex meaning and composite focus like "Deadly Ants" and "Intrepid Captive" in which the iamb and rhyming couplet flow with limpidity and felicity.

Another distinguishing technical feature of the poems is the accessible language in which they are written, tipped by expressions and maxims of rare mintage, a reflection of the poet's wide experience and heritage. The language appears invitingly simple but beneath the veneer of this apparent simplicity lie profound thoughts and intricate philosophies patterned in concentric circles around the unifying immanent symbol, Mother Earth or Nature. This archetypal maternal figure, the nexus overt or implied of almost all the poems, adds immeasurably to the structural unity and coherence of the poet's message: we note with empathy her tears of anguish coursing through most of the poems when her resources are rapaciously plundered or her offspring brutalized, trampled upon, left mangled or snuffed out by "Thorn Trees in Blossom", "Feral Flowers", "Deadly Ants", "Arrogant Belial" or heartless hit men at the service of leadership tagged as "Worse than a Dunghill". The poet displays a masterful use of the poet's shorthand – devices of compression, comparison, analogy and contrast – to which are added symbolism, pathos, pathetic fallacy, satire and rhetoric all mobilized as artistic vehicles and tools of expression for the besieged artist whose delicate sensibilities are confronted with a sordid socio-environmental reality that demands of him supernal courage in order to "Take a Stand", "Stoke the Fire" in him, "Mow Down his own [sublunary] Desires" to be permanently "Vigilant" if his green rage or "Words Should Shout [collective]Conscience Awake".

This is therefore a highly inspiring and interesting collection that recommends itself to the reader/audience on account of the breath and profundity of its current and timeless preoccupations, the engaging dramatic mood and direct poetic voice, the subtle blend of Horatian and Juvenalian barbs angled at constructiveness, a racy pace impelled by the poet's passionate feelings for the poetic trident (situations, subject matter and audience), the prophetic dimension which elevates the pieces to the realm of the sublime, and the whole couched in subtle language divested of decorative additions but which arrests in an intriguing way by "evoking a maximum of significance for a minimum of words".

It is thus certain that the poet has found in this artistic medium the spirit and an efficient brush and paint with which to clean and reconstruct the Augean stable – his society and the Universe – sadly bogged in the mire of selfishness, betrayal, corruption, cynicism, insensate violence and predatory tendencies on which thrive occultist coteries of global scale – the proven bane to equitable human progress. In fine, one finds in these poems a noble endeavour and spiritual mission aimed at refining "the collective human psyche" or raising of the "collective consciousness of human society" through the medium of carefully-wrought relatable mental images. In this way, hopefully, the lamentations of Mother Earth will be turned into smiles which will eventually irrigate her to produce "The Wealth of the Earth" for the common weal and humanity.

Enongene James Njume
National Pedagogic Inspector of English
Ministry of Secondary Education, Yaoundé

Beyond Recognition

The earth that once was so jocund,
never cross, never complaining
is today bowed in deep sorrow,
her shape defiled and disfigured.
Plastic bags and arrogant man
have stained and shattered her beauty.
Foul-smelling deadly waste choke her
and our darkening thoughts muddy
beyond recognition, her features.

The purity of green is gone,
the innocence of flowers soiled.
Forests are butchered for crude oil
but like bats we shriek with pleasure
and applaud in great excitement.
The petrol never gets to us,
tearing the heart out of the earth
that once was so jocund and pure
but is today in tears, filled with
everything impure and deadly
yet our darkening thoughts mangle
beyond recognition, her structure.

Vigilance

At the first light of dawn,
the ear strains to pick up
first, the strain of the earth
then the piercing woodnote
and flap of birds in flight,
away from traitorous roofs.
Thousands prefer to flee
rather than stay and strain
singing in no friend land
with nothing to boast of
where their afterbirths bleat
in the dust of the earth in tears.

The soul brandishes self
riddled with white bullets,
afraid to sing aloud
the songs it cherishes.
Foreign minds are hired
to chill millions of folks
for crooks to be chosen
and voted for to steal.
Truth is thrown to the ground
and trampled underfoot.
It is the writer's place
to stand with the oppressed,
not earth mothers, even in tears.

Misunderstood

I did not do the pools
to possess this black hue
nor draw lots to be born
in this part of the world
warm but misunderstood,
the hope of a new Earth.

Thinking the worse of me
is a gift not from God.
Maybe you chose your tone,
the earth's surface to dwell
and the tongue you now use
to tear my character
and cut down Africa,
the hope of time ahead.

I have tried to forget
the way you damn my race
and the mean theories spun
on our meagre headwork
but Reason refuses.
I did not choose my shade
nor my snubbed continent
the hope of tomorrow,
warm but misunderstood.
Could you be Earth's bad news?

Problem Child

Always, you sneak out at night
when the world snores dead tired
for the woods of mortal schemes
in league with nocent artists
with weed killers and nuclear waste.
The scared soil in sadness sighs
certain you will shave its head,
dig deep into its bowels
and bury your deadly kit.
You are the earth's problem child
fighting to flash to stardom.
Termites burn with love for you.

You are the earth's main problem child
always pumping her in excess
with potash and insecticides
for a better yield and harvest
to feed your greedy miscreant heart.
The soil is no longer fecund,
the spent ground muddy and bitter
and a raw pain tears Earth's inside.
You weep not though she is worn out
and the trees in her yard chopped down.
The Midas touch you have at heart,
to rid the earth of contestants
and have your roots deep in the soil.

Thorn Trees In Blossom

Out of the darkness thick
except for the stars pale
and a snore of anguish ,
the wind hums a new song
heading towards the south.
I try to weigh the strain
and the wreck on its prey.
The earth sighs for the unborn.

Night birds by their tempting charm
remind me I stand to lose
where darkness stands to be king
and fissures leap to the sky.
I try to ignore the threat
and pretend it is a dream
filling the holes in my brain.
I will be no Hamlet though.

It is the actual world in red
hidden from you and the eyeless.
There are thick thorn trees in blossom
where the heart hungers to settle.
I shun to think of the upshot
when the magma in our crania
and the rage in your hearts explode.
The earth will beat her breast in shock.

The Tears Of The Earth

Selfless Earth bleeds everyday
torn by man in his mad bid
to dominate the whole world.
The tears cannot be counted;
they draw deep tears from nightjars
but eagles are not bothered
and scholars in silence sulk.

My heart is sore with sobbing
but hatchet men flit about
and murderers fill their vats
smug with the blood of the earth.
Trees bend weary and thirsty,
bees and butterflies burn out
under the harmattan heat
at daggers drawn with mankind.

The tears of the earth are deep,
deeper than grief and the deep
refusing to share man's guilt.
Nature understands Earth's plight
from flowers without fragrance
and resolves to call the tune,
determined to heal the earth
and welcome earnest sane souls
in love with grain plants and blooms.

Lament For The Earth

I love to struggle up hills
and sit down at the summit
where the grass is below par
stunted by winds in protest
against the tears of the earth,
there to lament with the winds.
It may seem foolish when I
try to stitch songs from silence
to the gashes of the earth,
watching closely the blue sky
struggling to soothe bleeding earth.
The sane world weeps with the sky.

I cannot sleep for the best
when I think of the breaches
and the breakdown of the land,
down from restorative heights
and cannot cherish blade minds
fighting to tear up the land.

If you refuse to lament
and bleed for the earth in tears,
she will remain as silent
as a stone when you are flat
like an overused battery,
when a new order is born.

The Wealth Of The Earth

Even though earthworms sulk still
and streams groan under garbage,
even though the sky is sullen
and the environment thick
with the fog of pollution,
I will shade green with pleasure
the shaven head of the earth.

Even though earthquakes multiply
and windblown sand and dust double,
even though the oceans grow wild
and the nucleus of the earth teems
with the magma of malcontent,
I will without watching the sky
plant nothing but life-giving plants.

The world may battle with breakers,
the cockroach with worms and geckos
dreaming in the moonless darkness
dreams that will never change their lot.
I have unearthed under fruit trees
the wealth of the soil in full bloom.
The world can battle on with tides
and tear the limbs of earth for fame,
I have unearthed the wealth of Earth.

Feral Flower

The wild flowers beside you
sprouted while you were asleep.
Now that they have taken root,
you spin a web of white lies
in a bid to clear your name
and move away from reproach.

Day by day you boost your blood
with palm wine foaming like ale.
Now that it has crammed your mind,
you hiss like a puff adder
in an attempt to knock flat
all those who challenge your views.

Thinking of your spleen scares me
when far in the sea I see
the limbs of your foes floating.
I doubt Earth will forget them
even when your thorny tongue
leaves abscesses in my heart.
You are a feral flower
sending deep your deadly roots
for your young shoots to grow stout
and choke beautiful flowers
just as in your crazed fury
you tear all your adversaries.

Deadly Ants

A couple of red ants mate
at a geometrical rate
on blood saturated ground,
near where poets often turn round
before reaching their hideout
where they always have a tryout
in the quiet of the place
to sing better in life's race.
Sometimes they are forced to guard
the way into their own yard.

The deadly ants have increased
fronting even the deceased.
The splendour of this nation
no more stands in the station
where tourists often savoured
her plantain chips well flavoured.
We have character enough
to confront with rebuff
these foul ants gnawing their way
into the sack of our stay.
Make sure these ruinous ants
do not crawl into your pants
lest your dreams be castrated
and dumped upon Earth ablated.

Welcoming Nature

The splendour of the hills
and the breeze from the lake
soothing like a caress
open their arms to me
whenever I stop off.
Not so the human being
so aloof so big-headed.
I wish sweet Earth were wholesome.

When hibiscus flowers
beside hummocks flower
and dandelions blossom,
I see love in their eyes
with bliss pure and dove-like
wooing butterflies and bees.
Not so the human being
so selfish so conceited.

Mother Earth weeps and sighs sore
for her sons always at war,
not ready to hear the sound,
the sweet sound of whispering winds
calling on all those fighting
to lay down their arms and build.
Man has eyes only to kill
but lacks the tongue to restore.

Walking In The Woods

There is a kind of peace
when you walk in the woods
and loll on their leaved beds,
your head up on the trees.
Souls awash with hate genes
cannot breathe in the woods.

The woods are health-giving
when you enter them whole
and open wide your heart,
your mind in their green arms.
Hearts in the mud of greed
cannot stroll in the woods.

I have relished you since
my green season of life.
Even now that I limp
watched like a babe naughty,
I steal time to touch base
with you my pick-me-up.
In your fond shade I joy
sanguine, my livener,
borne like a newborn babe.
Walking in the woods free
takes a load off the mind
though the earth is hard pressed.

In Love With Deep Waters

I have loved deep waters
since I mastered breaststroke.
They sweep away fast waste
and sink all the burdens
likely to slow their flow.
Were you but a dreamer
walking the shores of hope,
I would teach you swimming.
The swift currents of life
you would swim through unscathed.
Deep deep waters assuage.

The planting season is past,
the grains saved have been eaten.
Elephant grass grows with zeal
where we were supposed to plant.
The cries of starving children
beat like a drum in your ears.
Were you but a musing mind
painting dreams in people's heads,
torn earth will bear unique fruit.
Flowers will grow on dry earth
and spread their fragrance afar
until the smell of rot dies.
Deep deep waters quench my thirst.

Bloom Close To My Heart

The seriousness of swallows
swims in the pool of my psyche
directing me to the Kurds.
Close to my heart is a bloom
I like to smell before sleep.
The Kurds may quicken my fate
or galvanize me to weep
in the zone of what I hate.
War may destroy my bloom's gleam
and drive those who hate her fete
while the earth torn, yells in tears.

The honey of truth when spilt
makes a bed for bitterness.
Robbers mystics hangmen split
stubborn skulls in eagerness.
We wade through mire and rot,
my beautiful bloom and I
half dead, clinging on shadows
like animals to be shot
and thrown where the road narrows,
cuffed, running the course of life.
I am tired of thrusting
my way through maddening crowds,
fingers clutching tight the ground
where wounded hearts in tears fell.

Your Heart's Trademark

The dampness of the night benumbs,
the haughty look in the moon's eyes
and a mouse groaning in a trap
somewhere in the kitchen outside,
the owls singing a chilly song
and hyenas howling together
somewhere neighbouring their stronghold
invite gravediggers to a feast.

Maggots awake from their soft beds
beneath a blanket of cold flesh
consigned to the earth the week after
 the last bloody student rising.
A benevolent but scared soul
lingers around the dreary place
bewildered by the shocking sight
and the insensitivity,
the callousness, your heart's trademark.
The repellent challenging scene
recalls the way dictators feast
and politicians drown their foes.
The stars and the moon sigh for love
where blood-begotten imbeciles,
the plague of this lovely country
have built on the dreams of loved ones.
The earth dissolves in tears troubled.

Best Ever Friend

Stunning woman, lovely fruit tree,
beside the once inviting lake
surrounded by engaging hills
in the bosom of the grasslands.
Gentle Earth weeps gently, troubled.

The lake that once gratified,
now terrifies like dark clouds.
Stunning woman, standing tall
with fruits and love in your eyes.
I will lay still my thick head
on your warm softhearted laps,
wearing green on pale brown grass,
away from where nerve gas hit us.

Lovely fruit tree, far from the lake,
beside the virgin pastureland
wearing green for celebration.
Remember my heart in your boughs
bowing to the wind but not rent.
When I call to mind the distance
covered these many trying years,
the future turns wet and muddy
but stunning woman, lovely tree,
you impregnate me still with hope
best ever friend in a sick world.

Daring Woman

She burns like glowing embers
and my heart thumps violently
as she contemplates a slope.
A mushrooming restlessness
takes possession of the brain.
In a moment of madness
I decide to follow her
to the brow of the gradient
steep and badly eroded,
to understand her fierce rage
and if possible bend her.

I see vengeance in her eyes
as her tears flow down the slope.
Her nearest and dearest friends
all at once with her offspring
lost their lives here rounded up,
butchered and rolled down the cliff.
They dared to dissent with heads
jostling for space in our brains.
This is the stew in her heart
boiling for limb for a limb.
This is a hard row to hoe
for orphaned and battered souls
struggling to tear a leaf out
of this daring woman's tome.

Women Of Heart

They must have been touched
where resilience stops,
scarce women of heart
watching mauled Earth groan.
I see seasoned scorpions
scrawling down their address
in their blood in scarlet
under a blood red sky.
Anger drums them to fields
where only the brave come through.
Faint hearts cannot dissuade them
nor souls fallen through the cracks
in the walls of our meanness.

They are unequalled
these women of heart.
Bruised Earth celebrates,
keeping close watch on spies.
When monsters cross our path
and goblins threaten us,
I remember loved ones lost.
Amidst raging arms of self,
the women break through armed lines
to safeguard all unripe fruits
and hearts beating for the land.

Intrepid Captive

How terrible looks the land
once so peaceable and sweet.
How like a disabled hand
she stands unable to meet
the needs of her descendants.
She once was the breadbasket
of a realm once resplendent
now a deadly straitjacket.
Masons have kept her captive
since we became less active.

Rosicrucians and masons
will do all to strip us bare
then dump our clothes in basins
trimmed with cryptographic hair.
Remember we once were great
with the people of the Nile.
The world then hated our gait,
their stand now still draws our bile.
Mystics must not win the day
else we be doomed to bind hay.
Though the Earth is all torn up
and grief tails us everywhere
to beguile us stain our hands,
mystics must not win the day.

The Need To Groom

I am aware I wear down
consumed by the itch to groom
under a sky stark and fair,
tongues to swap places with mine.
They will bring around gone minds
and the hunt for blood may cease.
The Earth will stand up for them.

I know as I move forward
under the keystone of time,
Gorgons will from behind heights
venture to turn me to stone.
The three repulsive sisters
drive back from the gates of Thoth
those seeking wisdom to drive
deep deep deep to catch fresh fish
from the pond near Free Rein Park.

White horses rush to meet me
beside the crags at the beach
seething with rage not heard of.
They want to change the landscape
we have failed to make gorgeous.
I am not sure I hate them.
The Earth may no longer weep.

They Lie Mute

My mates lie mute in the graveyard
where in the darkness of midnight
naked, you go out of your way
and make love to Tutivillus,
rousing the wrath blood alone quells.

Their death dares me to carve their names
in graffiti red and yellow
on the walls of our memories.
Laughter is bitter in my mouth
burnt in the fight to hoist myself
high enough to move at leisure
like puffy clouds across the sea.

Periwinkle flowers do bud
and butterflies couple in peace.
The lilies below mount Gracious
hug themselves in the morning breeze.
The pride of our land, sworn writers
lie tongueless in the dust, nameless
and honeybees refuse to build
in the desert of our nature.
Self-sacrificing Earth mourns
the loss of such true blue flowers.
She needs them to bandage her wounds.

Fire In My Head

The interest of the nation
bars me from casting my spear
in any lie of the land.
I wake up every morning
to watch the sun rise slowly
until she begins to laugh.
When her laughter grows taller,
a fire starts in my head.
Unable the heat to stand
I sprint to the nearest stream
there the fire to tackle.

The fight that breaks out is fierce
just when Sol begins to set,
putting a rope round my neck.
The water course turns oily
as I ready my senses
to take a dive of relief.
How do I quench the fire
in my head or clear the oil
in the headwaters standing
between us and deliverance?
An awful wind is blowing.
How do I restrain the storm
about to catch up with us
in a world cracked and careworn?

I Pray They Understand

They rush out like soldier ants
but back away in the heat,
obscene omnivorous beasts.
At the scent of honeyed bread
they go down the road again
ready to denounce their own.
Recanters are worse than war.

I have thrown the truth to them
and shown them the path to take,
filthy voluptuous monsters.
The love of land compels me
to write and be the tumbril
to lead them away to weep
in the cave of retrospect
till the wind carries their tears
to the castle of the head.
How I pray they understand.

The country will breathe better
without these voracious brutes.
The deprived will sing with joy
and quench their thirst like a tree
growing in its native soil,
spreading its roots far inland.
How I pray you stand with me.

Torn Future

Whenever darkness falls
indignation grips him.
Intransigent scorpions
unleashed by dark forces
have torn Wahntong's future.

He starves to stab his foes
in the heart of the heart
and fly straight to the stars
but his heart has been baked.
Sacred cows will eat it.

Birds can keep complaining
because of the wicked
who pluck the eyes of Truth
and never bend their minds
to the dreams of mind poets.

Clouds clad in sea colour
sail across the sky sad.
Sackers throng the streets red
to keep heartless power.
Wahntong has not buried
the hatred and the hump
he has for shuffling tongues.
The Earth cracked dies for him.

The Man Dying

1

He coughed long and spat
thick rheum mixed with blood.
His heart sighed and sighed,
dancing its last dance.
He seemed to remember
his mother's tender arms
but she was deep asleep
in the hands of the earth,
free from the sting of scorpions,
free from the world's troubles.

He took a few strides
towards a new pit
before him silent,
wondering why he lived.
His eyes rolled in prayer
but one humourless crow
sang about wolfish death
near an august graveyard.
He turned to return home
before the dead of night.
Earth blushed, let fall a tear
torn by guilt and censure.

2

The man coughed again
and spat lung slices.
My heart followed him

the spent man dying
but was locked outside.

He howled in his heart
trembling like a dry leaf
and sighed for the last time.
Dream upon dream collapsed
and the stars looked away
as he waited for death.

I left crying with rage
my mind struggling to clear
the thick fog before me.
The wind chanted softly
behind my back, a song
about dreams to be left
standing naked at dusk.
I hate the breath of pain
and the sobbing of Earth
overwhelmed by the blood
in the eyes of her kids.

Confused

The sky is blacked, the streets bare
and the hard to please in my blood,
the dreams buried along the way
and the tears shed in hot water
cultivate vengeance in the heart.
I do not know whether to smile
and water it day in day out
or knit my brows and break its neck.
The land has had a lot of kicks
and the earth is worn out weeping.

There is a worrisome longing
and a strange gander in my mind,
an accursed impertinent soul
I try to let go but cannot.
The eye of my roots are on me
searching uneasily for knives,
pacified by the thought of blood.
I cannot stand against the storm
brewing from the depths of the land.
A falling star tells me beware.
The earth, even in tears welcomes
the storm bred in the Atlantic
dead to excuses and feeling,
about to sweep across the land.

Unfading Fog

How long will the fog last
so we can lay our heads
on the laps of the land
confident we will waken
free to sing the blues for Earth.

When will the turmoil end
so we can frolic free
like squirrels in the grass?
Why do you sit silent
when serpents sink their choppers
deep deep down our yawning hearts?
You and the fog fit closely.

Unnoticed flowers die
in the unfading fog
vitiated by night worms.
I am out of my head
in this persistent fog,
my every branch cut down.
Maimed mothers mourn their beloved
battered in fields of repair.
The way Earth groans in the fog
since vandals waged war on her
under oath, I fear more tears.

Puzzling

The seeds from the soursop fruit
plucked when the wind was tempestuous
sprouted in teeming rain at night,
caroused with the light in the day
and enkindled hope in my heart
when the stars flooded the heavens.

The seeds burgeoned out steadily
into saplings fair and fecund,
bore fruit in and out of season
and birds of every hue and clime
wing their way in to have a feed.
None of my seeds are picking them.

The hope given suck to has slumped
and implanted tears in the head.
I have nothing but the dead leaves
and the harsh music from these trees.
They take pleasure in thrashing me
when the weather chooses to smile.
It seems that I must let go funk,
choose a brand-new environment
for sanctuary until my head
in the quietude of the night
can have something solid to chew
to calm the sourness in my soul.

Our Shame

Beside the drowsy town of Wum
where the hills ascend and descend
green with grass that engages one
with their intertwining music
sits inscrutable lake Nyos calm.
She looks so innocent and chaste;
the wind plays on her ashen bed
while part of me pores over her,
the other part wanting to drink
from the silver cup in her hand.
Death I hear does business with her
yet I want to fathom her still.

I just want to sit on her chest
when the wind bursts into pop song.
I want to go deep in, in song
when night tumbles and owls cry out
remembering those who died guiltless.
I want to bring to light my roots
and stand them on the rolling hills,
thousands in the throes of stiff death
their fair names splintered like china,
their honour moaning in dung mud.
They are very close to my heart,
the struggling survivors our shame.

Darkness Stirs The Heart

The cravings of the day die down,
the fangs and the fury of night
glitter on their way to build up.
Darkness begins to stir the heart
after a trip through the body.
A gang of narrow minds breaks down
all that the soul has constructed
in the heat of inner fires
to keep the enemy at bay.

Feather brains gaze from behind bars
the mire of their foolishness
competing with them for a prize.
Power mongers with snaking smiles
stand ready to get what they want,
deification and submission.
With the plunder from the subdued
they fatten their mysterious gods
hopeful they would outlive the stars.
Chattering like psychotic Cain,
they agree on oath to keep on
smashing the faces of the poor
and tearing the laps of the earth.
Darkness stirs the heart under stress,
sand flies multiply at their ease
and flowers of no name wither.

Searching Stature

I saw him fly almost naked
into the dim campus screaming
for the world to fathom his plight.
I imagine the heart wicked
seated on silk smiling, dreaming
how to stay the course of the fight
to recruit other mad people,
attain his grand master's status
and then feed fools with illusions
in a world congested with greed.

Could it have been the freshman's blunder
or did the madness come just like that
from the towers of the Erudite?
Could it have been Ambition's wonder
polluting the atmosphere like fart
to make those in power expedite
the transmutation of simpletons
and market many more delusions?
I can feel the shock in your blood
and the huffiness in your veins
brought on by the Illuminati
in desperate search of stature
to swamp the spirit of Ethics
and hoodwink the upstanding heart
in a world stuffed with defacers.

The Reckless Man Of Law

Clothed with shame and disgrace
the reckless man of law
tries to tear off the page
where he could not stick by
the cause of the fettered.
He can no more retrace
the route he took to saw
our freedom call with rage.
The masters he swears by
shun him like festered fish.

I will never make friends
with people who gamble
with the lives of others
or lift their eyes in pride.
When my emotions beat
their war drums to the bends,
where the wretched scramble
for sweetmeat with burghers,
I rise to have them tried
where Justice has a seat
carved out of an old tree,
the pride and the treasure
of a people not missed.
They hated recklessness.

Worse Than A Dunghill Mind

You once were full of deep feeling
and fairness dwelt in your ceiling
until the weevil of bad blood
ate your leaves and robed you in mud.
Today you outclass a scarecrow
and like capital in escrow
delivered only at midnight,
you wait well-dressed without insight.

See, the season of smiles is gone,
the leaders of your sect have drawn
strange lines on the way to the square
where the people gather to share
the stress they go through to vomit
their chiefs in disgust and dammit.
Freemasons have stripped your reason;
they will soon stone you for treason.

The nationalist in you died
the day your balls and heart were fried
in the kitchen of a white guard.
To him you were a dodgy lad
conditioned in the school of hate,
moulded to be shot at night late.
You are worse than a dunghill mind
living off the heads of the blind.

Target Of Hitmen

The colour of your eyes
is like the skin of rice.
I see in them bondage
and the fear of carnage.
Reduced to servitude
you sing in solitude
the fate of your kinsmen
in the net of hitmen.

The window of my heart
is open to your art
brimming with blood and tears,
aching for bright-eyed years.
The loathsome beast of lies,
empty head in the skies
sits up late stalking prey.
Bear with me if I stray.

Turbulent as the sea
the mind hears not the plea
of the heart ruled by greed.
I can't water the seed
of bitterness and strain
sown by some slipshod brain
enthralled by high office.
I fear lots of losses.

Arrogant Belial

The tussle in the dung room
in the neighbourhood of blues
between a rat and a cat,
the sea and full moon in love
and the ants clambering home
after a strenuous day's work
bring to mind man's level best
to make meaning out of life.
My heart goes out to the ants
and the earth knocked out of shape.

Arrogant Belial tramps on,
his stooges under his feet
in the neighbourhood of gold.
Daybreak brings for them horror
and youths with mournful voices
plead to keep their souls alive.
Nothing satisfies a dunce
ravening through garbage, doomed
like a written off lover.
At the beck and call of all
he flees from himself to live.
Arrogant Belial strides on,
oblivious to the tussle
in the dung room and the ants
clamouring for our support.

Rust-Eaten Nail

Life under a bald boulder
far from a spotless springhead
you seem not to have tasted.
Fake poets must be blamed for this.

You have never taken time
to sit and chuckle with us
nor ever dared your nature
to understand our lean lives.
The wind blows its nose nonplussed.

How my heart in earnest yearns
to cast your lungs in acid
on a day dripping with sweat.
You are the rust-eaten nail
long driven into our minds.
The puncture is yet to heal.

Take off the crown from your head;
let it be torn or locked up
till the tears of Earth run low
and the snake in your heart dies.
Man and boulders can be hard;
the fertile mind of Nature
will someday in scorn, break them.

Take A Stand

When you feel like a captive
and want to strip your heart off
the stone stocks of throes and shame,
raise your spear against death's head.
Take your stand on the mountain
overlooking the green fields
bounded by deep, silent streams,
without falling like a knave
at the feet of foreign gods.

Living away from yourself
in the arms of the desert
where no song can please the sun
kills the keenness to drive you.
Thoughts of walking out on you
have of recent rapped sharply
on the window of my mind
like a desperate spirit.
I want to hear from the birds
the best poem to write for you.
Take your stand on the pathway
away from the Cobra's base,
under the light of the moon
into any empty plot
to replant uprooted blooms
and give your kind a new name.

Stoke The Fire

Do not stretch too far well-wisher
to get to the root of the stench
in the air, of mouldering mores.
When we discerned the knacker's blade
and scented tear gas with wood smoke,
we knew wild dogs had been let loose
to begin tearing at teen flesh
like every bloodthirsty creature.

We never caressed the tiger
nor woke the fire within us
when the executioners came.
Like a widow broken with grief,
we began to trade our lifeblood
for a mouthful of bitter bread.
Covered with a wrapping of shame
the lingering flame in us died.

I have come out of the ashes
to stoke the fire within us.
I have come out of the ashes
to make you feel beyond the pain
piercing through the lobes of your brain.
Sunrise will water our dry roots
and the notes from my flute like shafts
run Earth's uncontested foes through.

Desires To Mow Down

Fire Francis to his senses,
seated on the Bermuda grass
beginning to grow beside you.
Lead him up the road to return
without delay to his birthplace.
Nothing crushes the mind of self
more than greed a sane soul murders.
There are desires to mow down
on the way to understanding.
There are desires to feed fat
when darkness dogs your every step.

We spend too much time on trifles
while the breath of youth is snuffed out.
We want our heads to touch the clouds
and our egos to seize the throne
without the fire in our blood.
If we cannot see beyond hills,
how can we rescue the falling
in a land where the earth has sunk?
If we cannot retrace our path,
how can we escort the blind home?
Fire the fire within you
to down the beast of anarchy.
There are desires to mow down
on the way to enfranchisement.

Wear The Right Garments

Let us stay on as we are,
souls seeking justice always
with our reason unfettered.
Let the distance between us
and the tears the earth has shed
for a very long time now
not drive us to strange waters.

I have learnt to cherish you
though the earth rails you for rape.
Red people have put a wedge
between us and the sound world.
I fear the worse to happen
now that flowers wither fast
and mad people fill the streets.

Let us wear the right garments
and sit down all together
to listen to age-old songs,
songs that can fly you and I
out of this torn grim terrain.
If I am false, savage me,
bury my fragmented heart
at the foot of the fruit tree
near where two streamlets converge
and hillocks kiss each other.

Too Glad To Leave

It will hardly leave the mind
the past draped in red garments.
I have done all to drown it
but it keeps resurfacing,
especially when I scan
photographs of bane and grief.
I will be too glad to leave
when the tears of the earth heal
and you no longer tear down
the repute of forthright souls.

I will not mind driving out
where the strong arms of the wind
will clutch me like a lover
to end shame and forget storms.
Forget-me-nots will bewail
the departure of a friend.
I often dash out at dawn
when it is their blooming time
to shake their motley fingers.
The painful waiting in doubt,
deep in the season of thought
clouds the splendour of the hills.
I will be too glad to leave
when the earth no longer wails,
when life can stride out and laugh.

Sighting Deserted Home

At the sight of deserted home
my soul my being search in tears
the location of our earth huts.
Life overtook us like a storm
and like soldiers in uniform,
we left the village not to fight
false fronts and whited sepulchres
but the stigma of slender means.

We staked our lives but lost the war
and like a whirlwind, frustration
swept over us obliging us
to go cap in hand day-to-day
not to be reduced to nothing.
We never wished to be hurled down
like pebbles or broken benches.
We chose to wend our way back home.

We go all out to fill the holes
where souls in the dark have fallen,
their tears dripping like a fountain.
The land will make us get better
shaving her head painstakingly
than go after ill-gotten gain.
Having gleaned grey matter from grief
we must back the cause of the weak.

Do Not Back Off Mate

Shutting the door to freedom
should not make you back off mate.
The womb of time will show zeal
the way to hammer off chains.
Come with me to the garden
though mother Earth is in tears
and the environment bleak.

Until the last flower dies
and the moon denies shining,
I will continue to strive
imperfect but on my toes.
Someday I will dig my psyche
out from the miasma of shame,
out from shoddy husbandry.

There will be people someday
with minds that forget nothing,
minds moving, masked like the wind.
To sleep on gravel is hard
behind a fort of terror
and forests dark as the night.
Shutting the door to freedom
should not make you back off mate.
Mango fruits ripen and fall
and everything has an end.

A Little More Patience

This abnormal reclaimed land
swallows all that sprouts on it
and allows no bee settle
in the neighbouring farmland.
Mother Earth raises her eyes
onto the labouring mass
growing weary of the pains
they have battled with since birth,
bearing with great fortitude
the strokes of appalling fate.

Surely the earth will lay bare
the hands ever shedding blood
upon her free friendly bed.
Let not your bravery break
like a termite-eaten tree.
Let not your fortitude fall
like a rotten mango fruit.

Just a little more patience
red-blooded labouring mass.
The earth will unmask the fools
ever stopping at nothing
to root up flowers they hate
or acquit the convicted
for the embrace of a bribe.

Road Without End

You have named estates after you
washing your kleptomaniac hands
with the blood of Earth's savaged face.
I have been following the sun
from where it wakes to where it sleeps
since I began using my head.
I still use it today though drained
struggling to talk devouring beasts
out of their ensanguined holdings,
away from a road without end.
Do not let power enslave you.

We can make woebegone hearts sing
the song of their truncheon journey
without their eyes filling with tears.
Let us not be like guava trees
stripped of their unripe fruits and leaves.
Mingling together day by day
we will strike fear that reconciles,
knowing it is us who agreed
bound to the earth to the last breath
to follow a road without end.
We must not let greed entrap us
under the roofs of men of means
not far from the road without end.

I Deserve Your Roasting

Indeed I deserve your roasting
from when I waged war on the earth.
Ants crowd my crypt day after day
declaring I have wrecked the land.
If I could set the timepiece back
I will bend low to the ground
and let the earth sequestrate me
or call on pikes to pick my eyes
and fill my mind with pumice stones.
I wanted to break with the past,
change the face of forbearing earth
and plant deep in your heart bloodlust.
Truly, I deserve your roasting.

Now I ache for the touch of trees
not for charcoal, not for coffins
but for the healing of the land.
The Earth still weeps for her children
lost in the forest of bad blood.
I harboured no thoughts of violence
till my neighbour pissed in my eyes.
The way forward dimmed, darkness puffed,
the earth though drenched with my misdeeds
still spreads a green mat before me.
Now I ache for the smile of blooms
opening wide their arms to me.

They Share The Earth Inglorious

They both share the earth inglorious
Power and Pride Earth's ransackers,
their ostentation and greed gone,
their authority with them too.
The selfless moon and the day-star
they no longer will link up with
when non-violence locates the heart
and torn Earth smiles satisfaction.

They sleep together in the earth
Sharks and Wolves Earth's problem children,
their jostlings for space sepulchered
with them in the depths of the earth.
The sharp tongues of ecowarriors
they no longer will contradict.
Their clash of egos rots with them;
the stars dance when wickedness dies.

Pests advance in ranks like locusts
to settle their kind in our psyche.
Skin-deep dons salute their progress
and fools trumpeting victory boost
the degree of our indifference
yet deep minds fail to denounce this.
Come, let us tend the soil as one
to share the earth in peace when gone.

Words Should Shout Conscience Awake

Words like seasoning spices
must be well chosen and ground
ere grilling to touch the heart
and nourish the wanting head.
They should also shout conscience
to man's senses unflinching
for our Earth to smile again.

We do not need to take flight
to strange lands beyond the seas
to be equipped with knowledge,
the knowledge to drown our greed
and mould an evergreen state.
We need to sound out our souls,
not bluff lives to disaster
nor pluck the wings of Reason
to kindle dangerous flames.

My vision is dear to me
though thorns are still on my way.
Pacing the trees in my yard
daily, dreaming up new words,
I wonder what your words build.
Words should shout conscience awake
to give us a human face
and bind the tears of the earth.

Out Of The Red Zone

It stands above all trees
symbol of love and release,
the age-old rugged tree.
I have cut down trees for warmth
and received gifts from friends
but the warmth and gifts last not.

It dwarfs all other trees
emblem of rare sacrifice,
the age-old rugged tree.
You can plant it in your heart
and keep your soul from ruin.
Nothing else can remould you.

I have left the red zone
sparkling with sweetmeats and wine.
I have left the bare land
dressed in a dress resplendent.
I have brushed off the world
for rest in the life to come,
away from this sickly earth,
this bitter earth all torn up.
You need to stop being cold
to piece together your life
draining to the dregs all thoughts
and airs that have the stain of blood.

Printed in the United States
By Bookmasters